TREE-HOUSE COMIX Proudly Presents

DOG MAN
MOTHERING HEIGHTS

WRITTEN AND ILLUSTRATED BY **DAV PILKEY**

AS GEORGE BEARD AND HAROLD HUTCHINS

WITH COLOR BY JOSE GARIBALDI

Published in the UK by Scholastic, 2022
1 London Bridge, London, SE1 9BG
Scholastic Ireland, 89E Lagan Road, Dublin Industrial Estate,
Glasnevin, Dublin, D11 HP5F

SCHOLASTIC and associated logos are trademarks
and/or registered trademarks of Scholastic Inc.

First published in the US by Scholastic Inc, 2021

Text and illustrations © Dav Pilkey, 2021

The right of Dav Pilkey to be identified as the author and illustrator
of this work has been asserted by him under the Copyright, Designs
and Patents Act 1988.

ISBN 978 0702 31349 3

A CIP catalogue record for this book is available from the British Library.

Printed by C&C, China

9 10

This is a work of fiction. Names, characters, places, incidents
and dialogues are products of the author's imagination or are used
fictitiously. Any resemblance to actual people, living or dead, events
or locales is entirely coincidental.

www.scholastic.co.uk

Edited by Ken Geist
Book design by Dav Pilkey and Phil Falco
Colour by Jose Garibaldi
Colour flatting by Aaron Polk and Corey Barba
Creative Director: Phil Falco
Publisher: David Saylor

CHAPTERS

MEET the CAST

DOG MAN: He has the head of a dog, the body of a man, and the heart of a HERO!!! He's lovable, brave, and enjoys chasing Squirrels.

STRENGTH: Kindness   WEAKNESS: Easily Distracted

PETEY: Once known as the World's Most Evilest Cat, Petey is now working on becoming a better version of himself.

STRENGTH: Intelligence   WEAKNESS: Easily Annoyed

LI'L PETEY: Petey's Son. He's a force for Goodness and Kindness, who lives with Petey during the week and Dog Man on weekends.

STRENGTH: Optimism WEAKNESS: Can Be Annoying

MOLLY: An amphibious Kid with a heart of gold and a propensity for silliness. She can fly and can move stuff with her brain.

STRENGTH: Psychokinesis WEAKNESS: Stubbornness

SARAH HATOFF: An Investigative journalist/blogger who fights injustice wherever it lurks. She's an immigrant from Australia and has a pet poodle.

STRENGTHS: Bravery & Brains   WEAKNESS: Impatience

CHIEF: The fearless boss of the local police department. He's got the bravery of a warrior, and the heart of a kid.

STRENGTH: Loyalty   WEAKNESS: Impulsiveness

80-HD: A friendly sentient transforming robot who is a loyal friend to Li'l Petey. 80-HD sometimes gets destroyed, but he always comes back for more!

STRENGTH: Creativity   WEAKNESS: Malic Acid

ZUZU: Sarah Hatoff's feisty Poodle who bites first and asks questions later. Actually, she doesn't really ask questions. She's a dog.

STRENGTH: Tenacity   WEAKNESS: Holds Grudges

NURSE LADY (a.k.a. Genie S. Lady, RN, BSN): Her genius ideas and caring bedside manner are world renowned. Her quick thinking saved Dog Man's life.

STRENGTH: Moxie   WEAKNESS: Chutzpah

GRAMPA: Petey's dad. He's a selfish, egotistical meanie who currently resides in cat jail. Petey and Li'l Petey no longer associate with him.

STRENGTH: Intelligence   WEAKNESS: Arrogance

BIG JIM: Grampa's pure-hearted cellmate in cat jail. Sometimes he moonlights as a superhero named Commander Cupcake.

STRENGTH: Cupcakes   WEAKNESS: Cupcakes

Thank You,
Randy Kessler

"...love is something eternal.
It may change in aspect,
but not in essence."
   —Vincent van Gogh

9

QUACK QUACK

HOLD ON, DOG MAN! I'm COMING!!!

Whitney Whitney Whitney

QUACK QUACK QUACK QUACK QUACK QUACK

HOSPITAL

CK QUACK QUACK QUACK QUACK QUACK QUACK QUACK

How is he??? Is he Gonna pull through?

QUACK QUACK QUACK

First, place your Left hand inside the dotted Lines marked "Left hand here." Hold The book open FLAT!

STEP 2:
Grasp the right-hand Page with your Thumb and index finger (inside the dotted Lines marked "RighT Thumb Here").

STEP 3:
Now Quickly flip the right-hand page back and forth until the Picture appears to be Animated.

(for extra fun, try adding your own sound-effects!)

O-RAMA

REMEMBER,

While you are flipping,
be sure you can see
the image on page **21**
AND the image on page **23**.

If you flip quickly,
the two pictures will
start to look like **ONE**
ANIMATED cartoon.

Don't forget to
add your own
sound-effects!!!

Left
hand here.

Right Thumb here.

Soon...

OH, NOOOOO!!!

DOG MAN! WHAT HAPPENED TO YOU?

He's okay, Chief!!! I Promise!!!

But why does he have to wear this silly Cone???

He only has to wear it for a few days!

But — but...

EVERYBODY'S GONNA MAKE FUN OF him!!!

Well...

I'm glad he has a friend like you.

You'll protect him, won't you?

Sh-sure I will.

Good! See ya later!!!

B-b-b-bye!!!

QUACK QUACK QUACK QUACK QUACK

31

How come you're wearing that thingy on your head?

Whine whine whine...

You did?

whine whine whine...

are you okay?

Whiiine whine whine whine whiiiine!

A Few DAYS???

Hmmm...

Don't worry, Dog Man!!!

33

You stay here and enjoy a cup of pretend tea.

80-HD and I will solve this problem!

C'mon, 80-HD!!!

FLip FLop

Let's go to the Grand ballroom!!!

FLip FLop

FWA

FWA

SUPa PILLOW fort

CHAPTER 3

ESCAPE FROM CAT JAIL

By George Beard and Harold Hutchins

Meanwhile...

Scribble Scribble Scrib

At Last! My Evil Plan is Complete!

I just need **TWO** secret ingredients!

Hmmm...

HANG in THERE!!!

Sorry, Grampa. I tried to warn you!

Only me and my new robot can use the Cupcake Exit!

THAT CARDBOARD HUNK OF JUNK CAN ESCAPE???

Well, it **COULD**- if I could make it work!

But I can't.

ON
OFF
EVIL GOOD

Maybe it just needs a battery!

OF COURSE!!! A BATTERY!!!

Meanwhile...

...while Dog Man was enjoying his pretend tea...

Lick
Lick
Lick

...Li'l Petey and 80-HD were upstairs in the Ballroom completing their new invention.

Okay, 80-HD. Let's test it out!!!

CLICK

48

49

We're all ready!!!

What?

?...

FLiP FLoP FLiP

FLiP FLoP FLiP FLoP FLiP

Fwoop

An Umbrella?

Good thinking, 80-HD!

We did it, Dog Man!!!

FLiP FLoP FLiP

Now all we have to do...

KA-PLiK

...is get rid of this thingy...

whoosh

...and replace it...

KA-Click

...with the **CONE OF DESTINY!!!**

Now any time you get in trouble...

...Just press the button on top...

...And all of your wildest dreams will come true!!!

Are ya ready???

Who's gonna save the day???

Is it **YOU**? Are **YOU** Gonna save the day???

GO SAVE THE DAY!

Oh, hi, Papa!

FLIP FLOP FLIP FLOP FLIP FLOP

DOG MAN

WHY is it THAT EVERY TIME I COME HERE...

...SOMETHING DANGEROUS OR OBNOXIOUS HAPPENS?

That's how we roll, Papa!

Are you ready to Go home?

Already?

Yeah, and You're coming, too!!!

Yay! You can play with me at Papa's house!!!

He's not Gonna be **PLAYiNG!!**

He's not?

No! He destroyed **THREE** walls in our lab last week...

... **AND** he broke our DooR!

FLiP FLOP FLiP FLOP

So I'm putting him to **WORK!**

CHAPTER 5
Bring On The Bullies
by George Beard and Harold Hutchins

Meanwhile...

COPS

Well, well, well!!! Look who's back!

Hey, MAUDE! Check out Dog Man's head Gear!

HAW HAW HAW HAW HAW HAW!

He looks even more RIDICULOUS than USUAL!!!

WHAT A DISGRACE!

WHAT AN EMBARRASSMENT!

WHAT A HUMILIATION!!!

You better hide behind that plant like you always do, ya **CONE HEAD!**

Yeah, **CONE HEAD!**

CONE HEAD!!! CONE HEAD!!!

64

cLick

KA·SHONK
BA·FLOMP
TRA·SKONK

BiBBidy BoBBidy BOOYA

68

No! Let's **ESCAPE!**

...er— I mean, Beep-Boop. Let's Go play **OUTSIDE...**

...and look for **Two** secret ingredients!

A TREASURE HUNT? Sweeeeet!!! What Shall we look for?

LiviNG SpRaY And Cannery Grow.

Why do we need **Them?**

Umm...

Hmmm...

...because cupcakes are delicious forever?

Makes sense to me!!!

Cupcake Exit ↓

DANGER

Danger

click

LET'S GO!!!

Cupcake Entrance ↓

Meanwhile...

PETEY & SON

Fix those holes first...

cement cement

...then you can fix the door!!!

Let's Go, Kid. It's time to take your **BATH!!!**

But it's **DAYTIME!**

Too bad! You need to get cleaned up!

Why? Because I'm Gonna be on **TV!**

Why? Because Sarah is Going to interview me!

Why? Because she's doing a news story about former villains who have transformed their lives.

Why? Because people like to watch stuff like that.

Why?

Because it makes them feel all warm and fuzzy!

Why?

BECAUSE iT TRIGGERS DOPAMINE RESPONDERS iN THE PEA-SiZED BRAiNS OF ALL THE GUM-CHEWiNG SiMPLETONS OUT THERE WHO'VE GOT NOTHiNG BETTER TO DO THAN THROW THEiR LiVES AWAY BY SiTTiNG iN FRONT OF A SCREEN ALL DAY !!!!

LAST WEEK you both spent **ONE WHOLE DAY...**

...Making up songs about **DIARRHEA!**

Oh Yeah!

HA HA HA

That wasn't strange. That was **HILARIOUS!**

NOT WHEN YOU DO iT FOR NINE HOURS!!!

HA HA HA HA HA

HA HA HA HA HA HA HA

CHAPTER 7

A Buncha Stuff That Happened Next

By George Beard and Harold Hutchins

Meanwhile...

SHAKA SHAKA SHAKA

MAYOR'S **NEW** Rose Garden **KEEP OUT** (especially Dog Man)

FWA

MAYOR'S **NEW** Rose Garden **KEEP OUT** (especially Dog Man)

BWOOSH

HOSPITAL

HUFF HUFF HUFF

PLUP

DiNG-DoNG

Oh, Look! A pile of slobbery roses!!!

I'll wash these off and give them to my patients!

That will cheer everyone up!!!

Meanwhile...

What do you mean, "No Longer Available"?

Well, Living Spray was banned due to complaints, right?

And they stopped making Cannery Grow...

...after the factory was destroyed in book #5, right?

THiS iS AN OUTRAGE!

Let's take our business **ELSEWHERE!**

Meanwhile...

Hi, I'm Sarah Hatoff. Welcome to my show!

Oh, hi, 80-HD!

Today we're at the home of Petey the cat.

As you may remember...

...Petey used to have a very bad reputation.

He was known across the continents...

...as the world's most evilest cat.

But all of that has changed.

Today, Petey is an upstanding citizen...

Be nice, Zuzu!

Yeah, be Nice, Zuzu!

Petey, just a short time ago...

...You were widely Known as a villain.

A ruthless bad Guy.

An evil, scheming, Good-for-nothing scoundreL!!!

But You've changed.

Yeah.

Tell me why.

Well, I—

IF YOU'RE hAPPY And YoU Know iT PoOP YouR PANTS!

PBBT PBBT!

IF You'RE hAPPY And You know iT PooP YouR PANTS!

PBBT
PBBT

If You're HAPPY And You Know it, then YOUR UNDERWEAR will show it...

...If You're happy And you know it

WOULD YOU CUT THAT OUT?!!?

I told You KiDS to Be QUiET!!!

How come WALLY's wearing clothes?

I WEAR clothes sometimes!!!

No you don't.

Well look who's here! It's Li'l Petey and Molly!

How are you two doing today?

fine.

Are we on **TV**?

Yes!

Testing, 1-2-3!

Hey, ya wanna hear a song about diarrhea?

No. We like potato chips.

ALRIGHT, **HERE!!!**

CRINKLE CRINKLE

SHUFFA-SHAKA
KA-KLAK
CRINKA
CRUNKA
KLOOPA
KLUPP

Do you got any of that white stuff?

WHAT White STUFF???

CRINKLE CRINKLE

CHAPTER #8

BECOMING

PETEY

Meanwhile...

Sorry, dudes. We're all out!

Cal 'n' Bunga's **SURF SHOP** And treacherous Canned Goods

I can't believe it!!!

NOBODY has Any Living spray **OR** Cannery Grow!!!

Let's do something else! I'm hungry!

NO! I'm **NOT** Giving up until—

...and a depot for doodads of **DOOM!**

HEY, LOOK!!! THERE THEY ARE!!!

ER, I mean, Beep-Boop. I have detected the items we were searching FOR.

We must Acquire them at PeteY's Lab!!!

...Your childhood was hard, wasn't it?

Yeah, but—

Your father didn't stick around, did he?

No, but—

And then you were orphaned.

Yeah, but—

But then something changed, didn't it?

ARE YOU GONNA LET ME TALK???

Certainly!

Okay, all of those things **DID** happen...

...but that's not **WHY** I became a bad guy.

Then why, Petey? Why did you turn to the dark side?

...Blew my under-

WHAT IS WRONG WITH YOU TWO???

We're thirsty!

Yeah! Potato chips can get pretty dry if you don't have chip dip.

No offense.

ALRIGHT, ALRIGHT! WALK THIS WAY!!!

123

BONK

Is that why you returned to a Life of crime?

What choice did I have?

No matter how hard I tried...

...**Nobody** would let me forget who I **used** to be.

Mean-while...

PETEY
&
Son

Hey, Robot! I don't think anybody is home!

Beep-Boop! Don't worry about it!!!

126

128

129

Left
hand here.

131

Right Thumb here.

NOW LOOK WHAT YOU MADE ME DO!!

Those Two Sippy Cups Just Came to Life...

...AND it's ALL YOUR FAULT!!!

Aw, don't worry, Grampa!

They're so cute and Little...

...What harm could they possibly Do?

PLink PLUNK KLUNK

CATCH

Shaka·Shaka Shake!

SSSSSSSSS

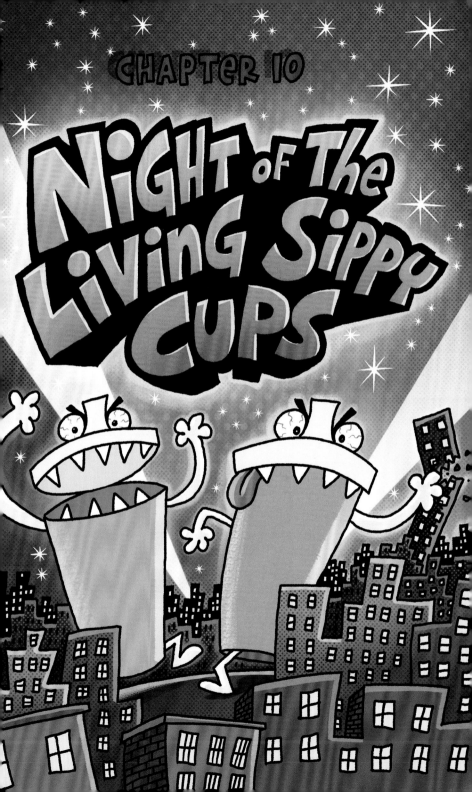

"DON'T WORRY, GRAMPA...

144

148

Meanwhile...

TAKE ME OUT TO the BATH-ROOM...

...TAKE ME OUT TO GO POO...

...MY Doodie Smells Just Like Rot-Ten eggs...

...And it's Starting To Run down my Legs!

Oh, if we don't get to the BATH-ROOM...

...And we CAN'T Find the dooR...

...There'll be ONe! Two!...

THREE Pounds of Poo on the BATH-RooM FLOoR!!!

WHAT iS YOUR PROBLeM?

Actually, we DO have to go to the bathroom.

Yeah. Seriously!!!

And so...

SiX MiNuTeS LaTeR...
FLUSH! FLUSH!

You kids better quit goofing around! It's getting late!!!

Where are we going now, Petey?

To where it all began.

If you really want to know why I changed from bad to Good...

... it all starts here.

This is where my Mom and I lived after my Dad left.

HAPPY HOME SHELTER
WHERE KINDNESS RULES

We arrived with almost nothing...

...and things were pretty tough.

BUS STOP

156

And then one day...

... When I Least expected it...

...her love became Something New.

That's me, right, Papa?

Yep. That's You!!!

I didn't recognize it at first...

159

161

162

CHAPTER 12
BIG FIGHT
chief
By George Beard and Harold Hutchins

HEY, YA BIG LUGS!!! LET GO OF MY FRIENDS!

HAW HAW HAW HAW HAW

ALRIGHT— YOU ASKED FOR IT!!!

Molly used her psychokinetic mind powers on the first sippy cup.

And it was working!

But the **Second** sippy cup got an idea!

Carefully it aimed its nose...

SPRAAASH!!!

168

169

I'll Never Get it Right!

But then... HEY, CHIEF!

Nurse Lady is on the Phone!!!

She says she needs you to—

COME ON, DOG MAN! NOW'S OUR CHANCE!!!

ZOOM!

Good Luck, Dog Man!

cLick

RAND·O·MON

O·MATO·PO

175

Right
Thumb
here.

While Dog Man duked it out with <u>one</u> sippy cup...

...the **OTHER** sippy cup was bent on Destruction!

HOSPITAL

HOSPITAL

CRASH

HOSPITAL

RUMBL
RUMB
Rumble

It's Gonna destroy the Hospital...

... and there's no time to EVACUATE!!!

You Know what we must do?

The struggle raged on...

...until things got really whack...

WHACK

...And Dog Man took the plunge.

SPLASH!

Sizzle Sizzle Sizzle Sizzle

THEN... HEY! What happened to DoG Man's Robo-Suit???

PLUP

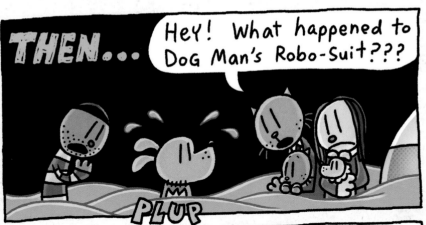

It's the Malic acid in this Apple juice!

It must have corroded his electro-Gizzards!

DARN YOU, Apple Juice!

Who's Gonna Save us **NOW?**

Meanwhile...

I've got to find a **WEAPON** or something!

But everything here is **BROKEN!**

Even this meerkat robot has lost her head!!!

But wait—

I can move her body with my mind!!!

Maybe all she needs is a **NEW BRAIN!**

Swooooop

MECHA MOLLY is GO!!!

So anyway...

Well, that was...

...Violent.

Thanks!

Welp, Good night, everybody!!!

CRUNCH
CRUNCH CRUNCH

Hey, WALLY? This might not be the best time to ask...

...but can I keep this Robo-suit?

WeLL, SURE, MoLLY! WHY NOT?

AS You can See, I've JUST LOST EVERYTHING!

So PLEASE, HeLP YourseLF!

NOTES

by George and Harold

★ The musical interlude of Chief's dream (Chapter 1) is a parody of the song "The Greatest Love of All" by Michael Masser, with lyrics by Linda Creed.

★ Petey's red cardigan sweater and tie were based on the clothing often worn by beloved children's television host Mister Rogers.

★ On page 123, Petey is paraphrasing John 8:7 (NIV).

★ Petey's youthful "mistakes" and "bad choices" were chronicled in the graphic novel where he first appeared, *Super Diaper Baby 2: The Invasion of the Potty Snatchers.*

★ The title of Chapter 15 is the final line of the 1927 song "Stardust" by Hoagy Carmichael, with lyrics by Mitchell Parish.

★ This book was inspired by the two songs mentioned above, the quote on Page 6, and the law of conservation of energy (a.k.a. the first law of thermodynamics).

MeCHA MOLLY

in 22 Ridiculously easy Steps!

HOW 2 DRAW CHIEF + NURSE LADY

in (17x2)+8 Ridiculously Easy Steps!

(X2) Now repeat steps 1–17 to make a second Person beside the first. **BONUS POINTS** if You can make it look like they're holding hands. Awwww!!!

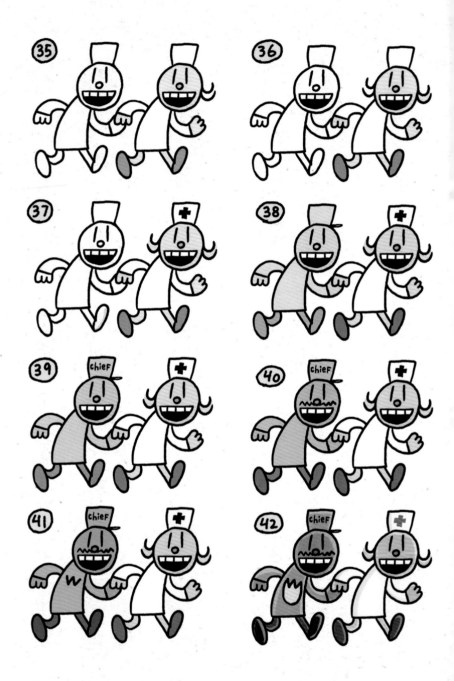

HOW 2 DRAW

The WORLD'S MOST TERRIFYINGLY EVIL SIPPY CUPS

in **26** (x2) RidicuLousLY evil Steps!

To draw the other Sippy Cup, Repeat steps 1-9 on the previous page, then continue here →

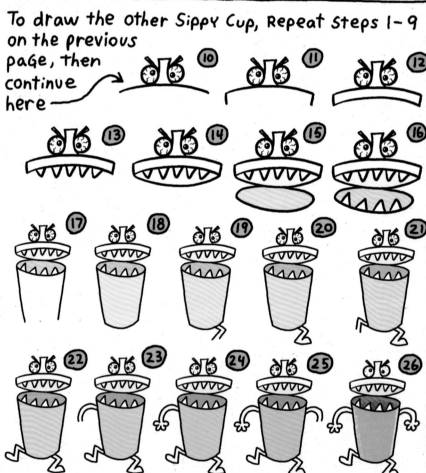

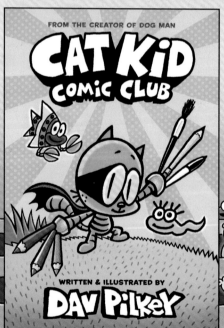

★ "Irreverent, laugh-out-loud funny
and . . . downright moving."
— Publishers Weekly, starred review

ER—I mean...

...Beep-Boop. Greetings, Carbon-based feline!!!

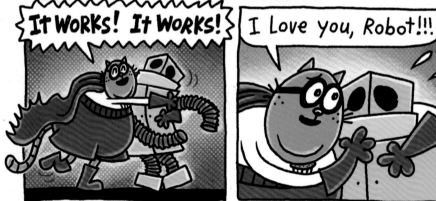

It WORKS! It WORKS!

I Love you, Robot!!!

What do you want to do first? Hide-and-seek? Coloring Books? Go Fish?

ABOUT THE
AUTHOR-ILLUSTRATOR

When Dav Pilkey was a kid, he was diagnosed with ADHD and dyslexia. Dav was so disruptive in class that his teachers made him sit out in the hallway every day. Luckily, Dav loved to draw and make up stories. He spent his time in the hallway creating his own original comic books — the very first adventures of Dog Man and Captain Underpants.

In college, Dav met a teacher who encouraged him to illustrate and write. He won a national competition in 1986 and the prize was the publication of his first book, WORLD WAR WON. He made many other books before being awarded the 1998 California Young Reader Medal for DOG BREATH, which was published in 1994, and in 1997 he won the Caldecott Honor for THE PAPERBOY.

THE ADVENTURES OF SUPER DIAPER BABY, published in 2002, was the first complete graphic novel spin-off from the Captain Underpants series and appeared at #6 on the USA Today bestseller list for all books, both adult and children's, and was also a New York Times bestseller. It was followed by THE ADVENTURES OF OOK AND GLUK: KUNG FU CAVEMEN FROM THE FUTURE and SUPER DIAPER BABY 2: THE INVASION OF THE POTTY SNATCHERS, both USA Today bestsellers. The unconventional style of these graphic novels is intended to encourage uninhibited creativity in kids.

His stories are semi-autobiographical and explore universal themes that celebrate friendship, tolerance, and the triumph of the good-hearted.

Dav loves to kayak in the Pacific Northwest with his wife.